Paleo Diet For Beginners

Amazing Recipes For Paleo Snacks, Paleo Lunches, Paleo Smoothies, Paleo Desserts, Paleo Breakfast, And Paleo Dinner

By: Ned Campbell

TABLE OF CONTENTS

PUBLISHERS NOTES

Disclaimer

This publication is intended to provide helpful and informative material. It is not intended to diagnose, treat, cure, or prevent any health problem or condition, nor is intended to replace the advice of a physician. No action should be taken solely on the contents of this book. Always consult your physician or qualified health-care professional on any matters regarding your health and before adopting any suggestions in this book or drawing inferences from it.

The author and publisher specifically disclaim all responsibility for any liability, loss or risk, personal or otherwise, which is incurred as a consequence, directly or indirectly, from the use or application of any contents of this book.

Any and all product names referenced within this book are the trademarks of their respective owners. None of these owners have sponsored, authorized, endorsed, or approved this book.

Always read all information provided by the manufacturers' product labels before using their products. The author and publisher are not responsible for claims made by manufacturers.

Manufactured in the United States of America

DEDICATION

This book is for my dad, who taught me to cook and inspired me to be curious and always ask the annoying questions.

This book is for Lucy, the Australopithecus woman whose fossilized bones taught us so much of what we know about ourselves and where we come from.

This book is for runners, bikers, and climbers; walkers, swimmers, and dancers; anyone who wants the energy to go further and be more.

It's for scrimpers and savers, do-it-yourselfers and guerilla gardeners, those who use their resources to maximum efficiency, and never stop repurposing until nothing is wasted.

It's for every bipedal hominid that has walked under warm yellow street lamps or cool brilliant stars to get home in time for dinner.

This book is to feed your inner adventurer and sustain the perfectly adapted and evolved body you call home. No matter your age, your background, your family or your situation, we all share common ancestors, and we all share a genetic code perfectly adapted to our natural resources.

This book is dedicated to the unique DNA sequence that makes you unlike any human that ever lived, yet nearly 100% identical to your 10,000-year-old ancestors. This book is dedicated to millions of years of breakfast, lunch, and dinner, before we even agreed on what to call them.

This book is for you.

Ned Campbell

September 2013

CHAPTER 1- THE PALEO DIET EXPLAINED

The Paleo diet is a more holistic and complete approach to food-related well-being than other trendy diets on the market. Many popular dieting plans are designed specifically for weight loss and center around the idea that the carbohydrate intake of the average modern person is far too high, causing weight gain when the body's natural processes store excess carbohydrates as fat. The starchy grains and refined sugars that contribute so much to a high carb intake are products of agricultural development, and also have a high rate of genetic modification. The Paleo diet removes entirely not only sugar, grains and legumes, but also dairy products, which were not in the 'stone-age' humans' diets.

The Origins Of The Paleo Diet

Pioneered in the 70s by a gastroenterologist named Dr. Walter L. Voegtlin in his book The Stone Age Diet, the Paleo diet is based on extensive scientific research that suggests that our genetics are simply not compatible with the carbs, trans fats and sugars that so many people's diets are commonly loaded with today. Unlike the omnivorous low-fat model of the typical caveman diet held by many researchers, The Stone Age Diet presents a robust argument for a Paleolithic human ancestor that was almost entirely carnivorous and survived first and foremost on animal fat, with very limited supplement from the vegetable world. The high-protein, meat-eating model held forth in Dr. Voegtlin's book is heavily supported by a comparison analysis of human anatomy, which has much more in common with the anatomy of carnivorous predators than it does with that of herbivores. Fundamental differences between carnivorous human anatomy and herbivore anatomy, from our teeth to our appendix, make it physically impossible for humans to ever fully adapt to a plant-based diet, and Dr. Voegtlin speculated that it is this inadaptability which causes a wide array of degenerative conditions.

Later approaches to the Paleo diet supported an idea of a caveman who ate lean meats low in natural saturated fats, such as fish and wild game, supplemented with high amounts of plant fiber and moderate amounts of monounsaturated fats that can be found in plant oils like olive and almond. Although there are a few different schools of thought regarding exactly what our evolutionary ancestors ate for lunch, everyone can agree on what they didn't eat. Whether the Paleo human chowed down on the fattiest parts of meat or had a nice salad instead, or both, Paleo diets had little or no refined sugar or salt in them at all..

The Stone Age Diet

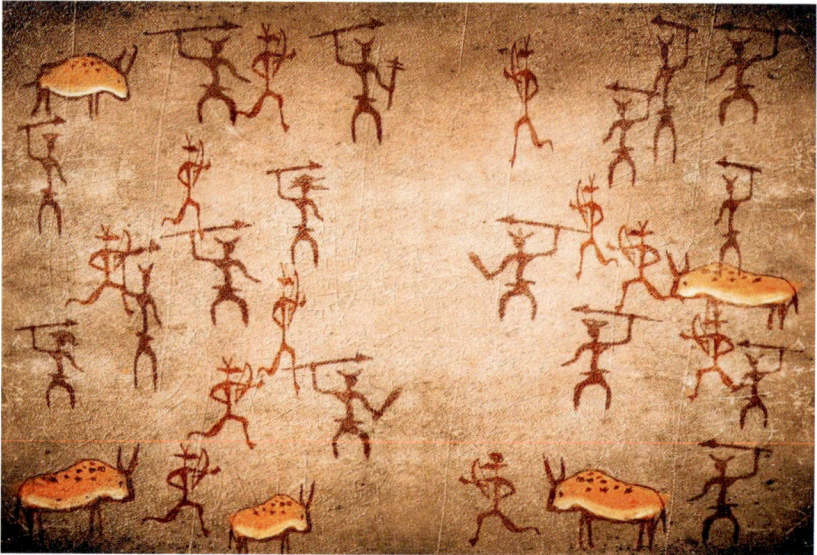

The Paleolithic era is one of the largest segments of human history, spanning millions of years. Also called the 'Stone Age', the Paleolithic era began with humankind's earliest use of stone tools, even before the homo sapiens species, and ended with the invention of agriculture about ten thousand years ago. Modern agricultural practices that provide a large majority of our food sources have existed for a relatively short time, and in the context of the long history of human evolution, have hardly existed any time at all. The Paleo diet is founded on the principle that we have a digestion system that is optimized for a pre-agricultural diet, and that the human body is naturally designed to most efficiently process the same foods that our ancestors ate. The development of agriculture not only made available new food sources that our bodies are not naturally designed to process, but also paved the way for centuries of genetic modification practices that, while they made food easier to grow, harvest, and distribute, did not make it easier to digest or make the nutrients more available for our bodies to use.

The principle is simple enough: don't eat anything a caveman wouldn't eat; but the effects can be profound and long-lasting. Historical and scientific evidence suggests that digesting and processing agriculturally produced foods puts more wear and tear on the body's entire system than consuming the foods we were naturally evolved to eat. The unnecessary strain that modern foods cause has been linked to weight gain, diabetes, and even other serious degenerative conditions like Parkinson's and Alzheimer's. Though many people who are mindful of their diets have the common sense to select non-GMO fruits and vegetables, many modern food sources, especially grains, have been genetically modified by plant husbandry to exist in forms that would never be encountered in the natural world. We have limited hard evidence today of how cavemen lived and what they ate, but thousand-year old tools and artifacts paint a picture of humans who mainly lived by hunting, and ate what plant life they could gather from their surroundings. While there is some evidence that the Paleo human did eat seeds, nuts, and other plant life, thousands of years of agricultural development have changed that food source into something the human body, barely changed at all, has not adapted to handle efficiently.

The Paleo diet is different from other popular modern diets in that it is not specifically designed to help you with losing weight, but rather to give your body the best and most usable nutrients without causing it any undue stress by eating things it is not adapted to process. The main goal of the Paleo diet is to optimize your body for long-lasting better hearlth, but this far-reaching benefit does help many people with obesity, cholesterol problems, heart disease, and other weight-related issues. While other modern diet fads usually treat only a symptom, like weight gain, often while putting other areas of your wellbeing at risk, the Paleo diet is based in your body's own common sense and promotes overall better hearlth. Many diet plans involve denying your body essential nutrients, and are so unpleasant and extreme that they can only be used periodically; this cycle of going from one extreme to the other can be ultimately dangerous, as neither extreme is good for you and it can affect your metabolism and energy levels, making achieving your optimum weight even harder.

The Paleo diet contains all the nutrients your body needs and promotes balance for a more sustainable and energetic lifestyle that is long-lasting and ultimately more effective.

What to eat

Though the Paleo diet may seem restrictive, ruling out cereal grains and dairy entirely, it's easy to have a delicious and diverse diet with emphasis on fresh meats, seafood, fruits and veggies. Just like any diet, it takes careful planning and adjustment, but your body will thank you for the valuable long-term effects. Unlike other diets that can deny your body nutrients that it needs in the name of fleeting weight loss, the Paleo diet allows you to eat all the foods you need, while providing the nutrients that stave off hunger and give your body lasting energy. Though dairy consumption should be limited, all other animal proteins, including red meat and eggs, contain nutrients that our Paleo ancestors needed to survive. Carb-laden veggies and grains like potatoes and wheat should be avoided, but a rainbow of root vegetables, leafy greens, and fresh veggies make Paleo salads a colorful delight.

Advocates of the Paleo diet recognize that fat is not the enemy, but that the healthiest fats come in unsaturated natural form. Delicious and unrefined oils from nuts and fruits like olives, walnuts, almonds, coconuts, and many others, can be eaten raw as a delicious dressing for salads, or cooked as a substitute to nutritionally devoid refined vegetable oils in your favorite hot dishes.

With the increasing popularity of the Paleo diet, there are several recipe books and meal plans available to give you creative ideas for how to make delicious meals from tasty Paleo foods. There are so many nutritious food sources in the Paleo plan that it is easy to tailor your eating habits to achieve your specific dieting goals, while still maintaining the Stone Age diet. If you are trying to lose weight, you can reduce the calorie intake in your daily meal plan, or if you are an athlete, the Paleo diet allows for a high-fat, animal-protien rich diet for lasting energy and faster recovery time.

The Paleo diet allows you to tailor your eating habits for more specific results and ultimate optimization, but a simple menu plan for daily living is an easy way to start building good habits, no matter what your lifestyle is. A good menu plan should still follow the recommended eating pattern of small meals with several light snacks during the day to promote faster metabolism. The following example is similar to the menu plans found in the bestselling cookbooks by Dr. Loren Cordain, today's leading expert on the Paleo diet.

Breakfast:

Mixed veggie omelet cooked in olive oil with a grapefruit and herbal tea. Add chicken or turkey to your omelet for an extra protein boost.

Lunch:

Mixed green salad with dried fruit, walnuts and avocado oil, lemon juice, olive oil or other favorite dairy-free dressing.

Dinner:

Spaghetti squash with pesto, garlic, and beef meatballs, with berries and honey for dessert.

Snacks:

Pre-cut veggies like carrot sticks and broccoli florets, prepared fresh fruit like apple slices, nut mixes, or slices of cooked meat all make great snacks that are easy to carry around and munch during the day, making it easier to stay committed to your diet. Convenient pre-packaged options like dehydrated fruit and veggie mixes or single-serving packets of almond butter are also available to make Paleo on the go even easier.

Why Go Paleo?

Because the Paleolithic era ended around 10,000 years ago, hard evidence of the average caveman diet is scarce. Though we don't have access to the history of millenniums ago, even recent history bears evidence of people thriving naturally on a hunter gatherer diet. A lot of information can be gleaned from looking at recovered stone tools used by ancient cavemen, and also from the historical lifestyles of peoples, such as Native Americans and Australian aboriginals, who continued to live without agricultural techniques well into the era of civilization. Before European influence, the vast majority of Native Americans belonged to nomadic tribes who never stayed in one place for long and relied heavily on the dense fat and protein of bison, venison, and seafood, with no access to farmed goods or salt and sugars. The image of the natural pre-European American is a robust individual with the energy and strength for a rigorous and challenging life. Very shortly after the establishment of European civilization and culture, native tribes faced obesity and other medical problems that illustrate a direct link to the sudden introduction of refined sugars, cereal grains, dairy and salt not consumed by humans in the natural world. This recent and rapid transformation is a case study of just how influential the correct diet choice can be on the well-being of not just individuals, but generations.

Though the Paleo diet often helps people with losing weight, and many people feel more energetic, this is just a beneficial side-effect to the true healthful power of Stone Age eating. Unlike some diets that focus obsessively on body weight, sometimes at the expense of other areas of your health, the Paleo diet focuses on using food sources that are optimized for your digestive system to reduce inflammation, degenerative disease, and all kinds of health problems that can arise from the modern style of eating. Research performed by Dr. Walter L. Voegtlin and many other prominent diet experts who built on his work suggests that non-communicable diseases such as diabetes and heart disease are products of civilization that were not suffered by our caveman ancestors. Many advocates of the Paleo diet claim that removing modern 'unnatural' foods from your diet can even help with depression, Alzheimer's, Parkinson's, and other neurological conditions that could be a result of consuming foodstuffs our bodies are not correctly adapted to handle. Many studies show that in addition to helping with these 'diseases of civilization', the Paleo diet provides a medicine-free cure for a variety of chronic digestion problems suffered by many people today. Colitis, Crohn's disease, chronic indigestion and IBS have all been easily and successfully resolved in a multitude of patients with a simple switch to the more natural eating habits that are part of the Paleo lifestyle.

Furthermore, many agricultural developed foods available on the market today are even further processed in ways that remove a lot of their inherent nutritional value. White flours and refined sugars most notably are made from parts of the plant that carry very little in the way of vitamins and nutrients, and your body does not even receive the full nutritional range of these already questionable plants. Milk and other dairy products are homogenized and pasteurized, removing not only harmful bacteria that causes milk to spoil, but also removing helpful bacteria that could help your body better process this modern food source. Even more extreme and advanced processing techniques give us high fructose corn syrup, isolated monosodium glutamate (MSG), artificial chemical sweeteners, and a wide array of other artificial or radically altered consumables that make snacking on a simple box of crackers like eating a science fair project. These nutritionally bankrupt food sources are often among the cheapest and most readily available, lining the shelves of the average supermarket in brightly colored packaging and making losing weight the less convenient option. Due to the ever-increasing availability of these kinds of food, more and more people seem to accept it as a fact of daily life that their diet has more in common with a laboratory experiment that it does with what the human species has evolved to eat. Even if you cut artificial flavorings, colorings, and other such substances from your diet, something that appears as natural as an ear of corn is the product of centuries of selective breeding, and is genetically modified beyond recognition as far as your digestive system is concerned.

The Benefit of Science

Many of the philosophies of the Paleo diet are based on the fact that human anatomy suggests that we are not effectively adapted to survive solely on plant matter, and that animal proteins are a far more efficient food source that was highly prized by our pre-civilization predecessors. Under ideal conditions, human digestion is the one of the most effective digestive systems on the planet, using virtually 100% of the nutrients consumed with very little waste. However, certain plant matter such as cellulose can't be digested by the human system at all. Animals that evolved to most efficiently survive on plant life developed a very different digestive system with anatomy and function that works on different mechanics entirely.

Dedicated herbivores like sheep and cows are often ruminators with multiple stomachs, requiring multiple chewing sessions and extra time in the digestive juices of the stomach to break plant matter down into its usable components to be shipped to the colon and absorbed into the body. Instead of grinding, chewing, herbivorous teeth, humans share the biting tearing incisors of other carnivorous predators, suggesting a healthy relationship with animal fats and proteins that is hardwired into our genetic code.

Just like a wild lion would be ill-adapted to a diet of bread and cheese, our primitive ancestors never encountered a bowl of cheerios in all their hunting and gathering travels. Although human civilization and society has come a long way since then, the basics of our form and function have not.

Though we do not have a lot of hard evidence of how early humans fed themselves before the invention of agriculture, a logical evolutionary science approach to health and diet promotes using food to assist your body's natural processes, rather than work against them. Indigenous peoples today who still rely on traditional hunting and gathering for the bulk of their food supply highly prize animal protein and fat in their diets, Inuit tribes famously valuing the blubber, skin, and vitamin-rich organs of arctic and sub-arctic animals. The hardy endurance of Inuits and other tribes in environments that are brutally hostile to plant life and agriculture goes a long way towards validating the claims of experts like Doctor Loren Cordain that state cereal grains, dairy, and other products of agriculture are not only unnecessary, but detrimental to a healthy lifestyle.

Like any diet change, joining the Paleo movement requires planning, commitment, and a little bit of sacrifice. Unlike other diets that are based on incomplete or symptomatic approaches, however, the Paleo diet is grounded in evolutionary science to work with the natural design of your body for the best possible results. More than a trendy weight loss fad, the Paleo diet is crucial to ideal digestion and overall well-being. A positive choice for any lifestyle, and adaptable to a number of fitness goals, the Paleo diet brings out the best in your body.

CHAPTER 2- THE PALEO DIET: WHERE TO SHOP AND PLAN MEALS

Caveman Diet?

As we have pointed out the Paleolithic diet, or Paleo diet, is a nutritional program centered around the diet of cavemen and women. This "caveman diet" consists of foods that would have been obtained by hunter-gatherers. Meats, seafood, fruit, nuts, greens, and other foraged or hunted nourishment makes up the core of the diet.

The diet is based on natural foods, specifically organically grown fruits and vegetables and grass-fed, antibiotic free meats.

Processed foods, sugars, salt, and processed oils are omitted from the Paleo diet due to their lack of health benefits and the fact that manufactured food does not fit the philosophy of the Paleo diet.

Vegetables and fruits are chosen in lieu of grains for fiber intake and a similar stance is taken with dairy. By following the

Paleo diet, mineral intake should be sufficient to ensure bone density without reliance on a regular calcium source.

The Paleo diet credo is that a simpler menu of natural foods will lead to better hearlth and an improved quality of life. The program is a drastic change from the diet of the average American but the potential for a positive lifestyle change, increased energy, and weight loss can mean the difference between a full, active life, and a sentient one.

Foods of the Paleo diet

Although some foods are banned entirely from a Paleo menu, others offer a multitude of options. Meat, fish, and seafood choices are extensive, as are the vegetables and fruits. However, there are limitations in seasonings, preparations, and forms in which certain foods may be consumed. Success with this diet will likely mean sacrifice for a dieter seeking a lifestyle change.

Dedication to the strict guidelines and practicing self-restraint are essential to properly implementing and sticking with the Paleo diet.

Eating healthier does not necessarily mean that eating more is acceptable. Even natural foods should be consumed in moderation.

Overeating or eating more than is needed simply because the food is healthier does not coincide with a diet paln for weight loss or healthier living. Habitual overeating or snacking will need to be stopped. Only portions befitting a dieter's physical needs should be consumed.

Once a good regiment is established and the diet program becomes routine, menus can be altered to some degree to accommodate different lifestyles. For example, athletes may require more starch for energy or weight-loss seekers should limit fruits with high natural sugar content. Each food category has it's own rules and specifications to follow.

MEATS

Meats listed on the Paleo diet include :

•Beef

•Pork (including bacon!)

•Poultry

•Veal

•Game (venison, elk, many others)

•Rabbit

•Goat

This list is, by no means, all inclusive. There is virtually no type of meat disallowed by the Paleo diet, excepting processed meats like hot dogs. There is no set limit on how much meat may be consumed while on the Paleo diet but with a protein-rich program, the appetite should be curbed to a degree, aiding in weight loss and calorie burning.

Preferred cooking methods for the meat tend to sway toward different roasting techniques, frying, grilling, poaching, or stewing. Depending on the cut of meat and desired outcome, some meats would fare better with certain cooking methods than others. Oven roasting and pan roasting are slow-cook methods and require quite some time. Stewing may also prove time-consuming but may be the best option for meat that needs long cooking times to become tender. Frying and grilling would be ideal for faster cooking and cuts of meat that don't need a lot of fuss.

For frying, use only an approved oil or fat (see below) and cook until desired doneness or required temperature. In the case of an exotic or unfamiliar meat, some research is suggested to discover the appropriate serving temperature that is considered safe for consumption. The same recommendation is made for grilling. Poaching is a method that is more suited to poultry or fish.

Though poaching may sound like a slow process, because the meat used for this method is already tender, cooking time should not be lengthy.

An alternative protein of the Paleo diet is the egg. Chicken, duck, quail, or goose eggs from organically fed birds are

preferred. Any cooking method will do and little or no fat is even needed for a good meal featuring an egg.

FISH AND SHELLFISH

If it's classified as a fish, it can be eaten on the Paleo diet. As long as the fish is prepared without breading, there is no going wrong with seafood as a protein. Shellfish are another wonderful source of protein and there are plenty to chose from:

•Shrimp

•Lobster

•Crab

•Clams

•Scallops

•Oysters

These gifts from the ocean can be prepared simply and easily and served plain, with a squirt of lemon, in a stew, or with a salad of leafy greens. Incorporating fish and seafood into the Paleo diet along with traditional meat, adds variety and Omega-3 to the mix.

VEGETABLES

Vegetables are just as important a component in the Paleo diet as protein. Vegetables provide scores of minerals and vitamins and the exhaustive list of veggies that are acceptable for this diet runs the gamut from leafy greens to root vegetables and everything in between. Raw or cooked, the cornucopia of vegetables on this list assist the dieter in achieving their goal of better hearlth.

There is a word of caution, however. Potatoes and squash are generally not included in the Pleo diet due to their high starch content and low nutritional value. As stated above, athletes may turn to potatoes to increase their energy levels and caloric

intake for exercise purposes. This would not be ideal for a person in pursuit of losing weight. In that case, it is better to stick solely with the vegetables on the Paleo list. Here's a sample:

- Lettuce

- Spinach

- Asparagus

- Celery

- Carrots

- Greens (any)

- Eggplant

- Beets

Technically fungi, mushrooms are also found in the produce section, so we'll include them here. Any type of mushroom can be used and mushrooms are an easy insert into almost any recipe.

Vegetables can fill the role of a side or accompaniment or can be eaten as a snack between meals. Many cooking options and preparations are available for any number of vegetables. Experimenting with this aspect of the diet could prove interesting and fun.

FRUITS

Fruits are essential to the Paleo diet but fruit should be consumed in moderation. Positive benefits aside, fruits contain natural sugars. While some types house more sugar than others, it is wise to be judicious when it comes to fruit intake. People attempting to lose weight should avoid these high-sugar fruits:

- Apples

- Bananas

- Cherries (sweet)

- Grapes

- Kiwi

- Mangos

- Pears

- Pineapple

Dieters suffering from insulin deficiencies should also restrict consumption of fruit and should consult a physician's advice before proceeding with the diet. Fruits lower in sugar content should be the main focus for weight loss candidates and medically compromised individuals. Low sugar fruits still contain sugar but not at the levels of the fruit in the above list. These other fruits include:

- Berries (any kind)

- Oranges

- Peaches

- Grapefruit

- Plums

- Cantaloupe

- Lemons and limes

- Watermelon

- Cherries (sour)

- Figs

Fruit juices should also be approached with a speculative eye because of very high sugar contents and/or high fructose corn syrup among the ingredients. Some dried fruits also have this issue. Read labels or make homemade whenever possible is a good rule of thumb.

NUTS AND SEEDS

Raw and roasted nuts and seeds are an excellent snack choice. Eaten on their own or tossed with dried fruit in a trail mix, these crunchy bits can add some natural fat to the diet. That being said, cashews should be eaten with caution, as their fat content tends to run high.

It should be noted that peanuts are not part of the Paleo diet. Peanuts are actually legumes. Legumes are beans or peas and are excluded from the diet because of their Phylic acid content. The acid absorbs essential nutrients before the body can benefit from the food, therefor rending the intake of legumes pointless and essentially empty calories. Acceptable nuts and seeds are:

- Almonds

- Pistachios

- Hazelnuts

- Brazil nuts

- Pecans

- Walnuts

- Macadamia nuts

- Pine nuts

- Sunflower seeds

- Pumpkin seeds

- Sesame seeds

Almond milk is sometimes used as a dairy substitute and can increase calcium intake in dieters. Avoid soy milk and other soy products, as soy is a legume.

OILS AND FATS

The Paleo diet promotes the use of natural oils and fats. Oils derived from nuts, olives, or coconuts are considered acceptable.

If grass fed butter can be found, this is another excellent source of fat. Alternative sources or oil and fat approved by the

Paleo diet:

• Avacados

• Sardines (and other fatty fishes)

• Clarified butter

• Fresh butter (unprocessed)

SPICES

A natural diet does equate to a bland one. The Paleo diet allows for the use of spices and herbs, both as a flavoring device and enhancers for vitamins, minerals, and nutrients. Dried spices and herbs can add color, flavor, and mouth-watering aromatics to a dish while fresh herbs can crank up the vitamins and minerals.

Nearly any spice or fresh herb can be incorporated into the diet but here are a few suggestions:

- Parsley

- Basil

- Thyme

- Cinnamon

- Mint

- Cumin

- Cilantro

- Dill

- Paprika

- Mustard seeds

A myriad of other spices and herbs exist and can be implemented into meat, fish, or vegetable dishes or even a dash of a little something on a snack item can add something special.

THIRST QUENCHERS

Water is encouraged for the Paleo diet. A splash of lemon or lime juice can liven it up a bit or tea can be substituted. Herbal tea, either black or green, is suggested. No milk or sugar added. Black coffee is acceptable as well. Drinks and beverages not included in the diet consist of:

•Milk (no dairy)

•Soda (of any kind)

•Fruit juice (especially store bought)

SHOPPING FOR THE PALEO DIET

When it comes to the more exotic fare, special grocers and butchers are probably the safer bet but not everyone has easy access to high-end products. Food shopping can be problematic due to location restrictions and budgetary constraints can limit what is purchased.

The best advice is: get what you can afford and jazz it up with spices from the pantry.

Buy the best meat and fish available without spending the whole budget on a single meal. Farmer's Markets and vegetable stands run by local farms can save money and offer quality produce. Shop conservatively, look out for sales and specials, and cater to your own tastes.

MEAL PLANS

The Paleo diet menu can be quite diverse even with it's limited components. Here is a sample meal plan for 3 days:

Monday

Breakfast: Spinach and mushroom omelet with 1/2 cup berries on the side and tea or coffee.

Lunch: Chicken salad with mixed greens and olive oil/lemon dressing. Water or tea.

Dinner: Grilled tuna with a side of assorted veggies and water or tea.

Tuesday

Breakfast: Eggs and bacon with orange slices and coffee.

Lunch: Turkey burger with cabbage salad and water.

Dinner: Garlic and herb pork tenderloin and steamed cauliflower with side salad and tea.

Wednesday

Breakfast: Fruit salad (melon, apple, berries) and coffee.

Lunch: Grilled beef kabobs with peppers and onions and grilled fruit (peaches or pineapple)

Dinner: Meatloaf with sautéed mushrooms and bacon.

Health Benefits of the Paleo Diet

Better health can be achieved through the Paleo diet. Losing weight and increasing muscle are just a few benefits to following the program. Studies have show improved blood pressure and glucose levels in practitioners and dieters speak of decreased intestinal issues and higher energy levels.

Without added sugars, fats, and processed foods, Paleo eliminates key factors in weight gain and diet-oriented health issues. By implementing smarter food shopping strategies, eating habits, and lifestyle changes, the Paleo follower can reap the benefits of a fitter countenance and a higher quality of life. r

CHAPTER 3- PALEO RECIPES FOR BREAKFAST, LUNCH AND DINNER

Delicious and Simple Meals, Snacks, and Desserts You'd Never Guess Were Paleo

The Paleo diet is extremely good for the body, mind, and soul; but for beginners, it can also seem extremely complicated. The recipes that follow will get you off to a great start eating Paleo style breakfasts, lunches, dinners, snacks, and desserts.

These aren't your run-of-the-mill recipes, either. Each selection is a restaurant quality meal, dessert, or snack that you can easily make at home, with ingredients that can be easily found at any grocery store.

So, kick back, relax, and get ready to eat some of the most delicious meals you've ever cooked at home, and smile knowing that each selection is getting you closer to a better diet, and most importantly, better health!

Delicious Paleo Breakfasts To Start The Day off Right

Indian Style Egg Scramble

•6 eggs, beaten well

•1 onion, diced

•2 garlic cloves, crushed and chopped

•1 mild chili, chopped and deseeded

•Spices: 1/2 tsp. cumin, 1/2 tsp. turmeric, and 1/2 tsp freshly ground black pepper

•a handful of grape tomatoes, quartered

•a handful of baby spinach leaves, chopped

•a glug of olive oil

•a pinch of sea salt

•and fresh coriander for garnish (optional).

Over medium heat, warm up olive oil and saute the diced onion with a pinch of sea salt until the onions start to caramelize, or turn a sweet golden brown.

Add spices, garlic, and chopped chili and continue to fry until fragrant, just 2-3 minutes.

Add the tomatoes and spinach to the pan, pouring the egg over all ingredients. turn the heat down to med-low to prevent burning and sticking. Stir frequently until the eggs are cooked to your favorite temperature. Dress with fresh chopped coriander, and serve.

Serves 2.

Paleo Eggs and Hash

- 3 tsp. coconut oil, divided

- 1 green bell pepper

- 1/2 medium yellow onion or 1 small, finely chopped

- 1 medium sweet potato

- 2 sausages, nitrate free (optional)

- 2 eggs

- 1 Tbsp. water

Over medium heat, heat 2 of the 3 tsp coconut oil in a large skillet.

Saute onions and sweet potatoes for approximately five minutes, then add sliced sausages, cooking until meat is browned and sweet potatoes are slightly tender.

Add green pepper along with 1 T water, covering to cook for 15 minutes -or until sweet potatoes are completely tender. Stir frequently during this step to prevent burning and sticking.

Fry eggs to your liking and serve over your Paleo hash. Garnish with freshly ground black pepper. Serves 2.

Fabulous, Savory Brunch Fruit Salad

1 ripe peach, peeled and diced

2/3 cup blueberries

handful of sweet, ripe cherry tomatoes, halved

fresh basil and parsley, finely chopped

Toss fruits together in a bowl and dress with either:

1/2 tsp. balsamic vinegar blended with 2 tbsp. olive oil or

1/2 tsp white vinegar blended with 2 tbsp. olive oil, and a dash of sea salt and pepper.

Sprinkle chopped herbs over the top and serve immediately.
Serves 2

Summer Vegetable Frittata

2 tbsp. olive oil (or coconut)

1/2 small zucchini, chopped

1/2 small summer squash, chopped

2 garlic cloves, finally chopped

A handful of grape tomatoes, halved and deseeded

1/2 bell pepper, any color, chopped

1/2 medium red or yellow onion, diced

Parsley, finely chopped

Thyme, finely chopped

1/2 tsp sea salt, divided into two 1/4 measures

1/4 tsp freshly ground black pepper, divided into two 1/8 measures.

8 eggs

In an oven proof skillet, preferably measuring 10", heat up oil over medium heat. Add zucchini, summer squash, pepper, onion, garlic, 1/4 tsp. salt, 1/8 tsp. pepper, thyme, and parsley. Cover and cook for 5-7 minutes, until veggies are tender. Stir every so often to keep the contents of the skillet from sticking.

Add tomatoes and cook the veggies uncovered for around 5 more minutes. Meanwhile, beat eggs in a large bowl with remaining salt and pepper until combined. Pour over skillet contents, stirring carefully.

Replace the cover of the skillet and cook on low heat for 10-15 minutes, until the egg has begun to set. Preheat the broiler on low. Allow the frittata to finish cooking uncovered, under the broiler for 3 minutes. Carefully remove skillet from the oven and

serve. Serves 4.

Easy Paleo Breakfast Casserole

12 large eggs

1 cup grape or cherry tomatoes

2 cups kale

8 slices center cut bacon

2 cloves garlic, peeled, crushed, and chopped

sea salt

freshly ground black pepper

1/2 tsp. tarragon

Preheat the oven to 375 degrees F. While the oven heats, cook bacon until it is no longer raw but is not crispy (it will need to be able to withstand heat in the oven without turning into shoe-leather).

Chop kale, discarding the stems, break up the bacon, and halve the tomatoes. place them into an oven safe baking dish, along with the garlic. Beat eggs in a large bowl. Blend in the sea salt, pepper, and tarragon. Pour the seasoned eggs over the ingredients in the baking pan.

Bake for 25-30 minutes, or until the egg in the center of the casserole has set and the casserole top is a nice golden brown.

Delicious Paleo Pancake

1 large sweet potato

3 eggs

1/2 cup coconut milk, unsweetened

2 1/2 tsp. cinnamon

1/2 tsp. nutmeg

1/2 tsp. sea salt

1 tsp. baking soda

1 tsp. baking powder

coconut oil for frying.

Peel, chop, and boil the sweet potato until it is tender. Allow it to cool completely.

Using a blender, combine all ingredients until a rather runny batter results, adding more coconut milk as needed if the batter is too thick.

On a hot griddle, over medium heat, melt an ample amount of coconut milk. Pour batter to form large or small pancakes, depending on preference. When bubbles start to form on the wet side of the pancake- approximately 2-3 minutes into cooking time - flip to continue cooking the other side. Repeat, using more coconut oil to grease the griddle when necessary, until all the batter has been used. Serve with eggs any style or locally harvested maple syrup. Serves 4.

Apple and Cinnamon Breakfast Smoothie

1 Tbsp raw, unfiltered honey

1 tsp. cinnamon

1 cup apples (tart varieties work well), chopped

1/2 tsp real vanilla extract

1 cup cold coconut milk

1/4 c. unsalted cashews

In a blender or food processor, pulse all ingredients until smooth. Serve with a sprinkle of cinnamon on top. Serves 2.

Unforgettable Salads, Sandwiches, Soups and Entrees For Paleo Lunches or Dinners (For Any Day of the Week!)

Arugula and Strawberry Salad

1 cup fresh arugula

handful of fresh strawberries, sliced

1/2 tsp. balsamic vinegar

2 Tbsp. olive oil

Toss sliced strawberries with the fresh arugula. Combine balsamic vinegar and olive oil and drizzle over salad for a light lunch filled with amazing bitter, sweet, and savory flavors.

Paleo Quiche

Preheat oven to 350 degrees F. Meanwhile, in a mixing bowl combine2 eggs, beaten and 1/2 cup melted coconut oil.

Stir in

3/4 cup coconut flour

and 1/2 tsp coarse salt

Mix all ingredients well until a dough begins to form. Press the dough into a greased pie plate. After making sure the crust is evenly spread within the pan, prick with a fork and bake in oven for approximately ten minutes.

In a large mixing bowl, combine

5 eggs, beaten

1/2 cup coconut milk

1 tsp coarse salt

dash of freshly ground black pepper

2 cloves of garlic, peeled, crushed and chopped

Over medium heat, cook

3/4 lb. good quality sausage.

Drain sausage with a slotted spoon, reserving the grease to wilt

2 cups baby spinach, roughly chopped.

Add sausage and spinach to egg mixture, along with

2 green onions, minced.

Pour the egg mixture into the pan with the coconut flour crust. Bake for 25-30 minutes, until the egg in the center of the quiche has firmly set.

Summer Salad with Watermelon and Cucumber

1 large seedless cucumber

1/2 red onion, finely sliced

4 cups cubed seedless watermelon

Sea salt

juice of one lemon

2 Tbsp. high quality olive oil

handful of fresh basil leaves, sliced finely

In a large bowl, combine salt, lemon juice, and olive oil t create a dressing. Add cucumber, onion, and watermelon to the bowland toss well with dressing. Sprinkle sliced basil over the top. Season to your liking with additional basil, lemon juice, olive oil, and salt.

Gazpacho

In a large sauce pan, bring water to a boil. Poach for 20 seconds

8 good sized fresh tomatoes

While rinsing under cold water, immediately peel the skins from the tomatoes, take out the seeds, and place the fruit in a prepared food processor.

Add to the food processor (or blender)

1 cucumber, peeled and chopped

1 red onion, peeled and chopped

1 green pepper, deseeded and chopped

1 red pepper, deseeded and chopped

3 garlic cloves, peeled and crushed

1 chili pepper, deseeded and coarsely cut

Juice and zest of 1/2 an orange

1 cup water (cold)

When these ingredients are well blended, add

3/4 cup olive oil

1 cup organic tomato juice

dash sea salt

dash freshly ground black pepper

2 Tbsp. cider vinegar

Quickly pulse. Serve immediately or chill in the refrigerator before serving. Garnish with diced vegetables and olive oil.

Old Fashioned Liver and Onions

4 large red onions

6 Tbsp. grass fed butter, divided

4 large liver slices (pork or calf)

Sea salt

Freshly ground black pepper

Over medium low heat, prepare a skillet. Sautee onions in 5 Tbsp. butter until they begin to caramelize and soften. In a separate skillet, cook the slices of liver in the remaining 1 Tbsp. butter, 3 minutes on each side, until cooked through.

Top the liver with the caramelized onions and enjoy. Serves 4.

Healthy, Savory Romaine Wraps

2 large romaine leaves

1 diced grilled chicken breast

handful of grape tomatoes

red and yellow pepper slices

sliver of red onion

1 Tbsp. olive oil

1/2 tsp. balsamic vinegar

sea salt

black pepper

Spread the romaine leaves out on the cutting board. In a bowl, toss vegetables and chicken together.

In a small bowl, combine balsamic, olive oil, salt and pepper, drizzle over the chicken and vegetables, tossing with a wooden spoon.

Spoon the mixture on to the lettuce leaves, and roll the leaves as you would a wrap. Makes a quick, delicious lunch for one.

Paleo Pizza

Preheat oven to 350 degrees F.

To make the crust, mix together

2 free range eggs

2 cups almond meal

3 Tbsp. good olive oil

1/4 tsp baking soda

2 cloves garlic, minced

1 sprig fresh rosemary, chopped

4-5 fresh basil leaves, chopped.

Form the dough into a ball. Grease a pizza pan with olive oil, and by using your hands, gently spread the dough from the center of the pan to the edges by stretching it.

Bake the crust in the oven alone for 20 minutes.

Meanwhile, in a skillet, cook together

2 small summer squash, diced

1 small zucchini, diced

3 diced scallions

a few ripped-up basil leaves.

When the vegetables are tender, toss in a handful of grape tomatoes, halved 1/4 cup sliced greek or black olives.

After crust has been removed from the oven, spread over it

1 cup marinara sauce and top with sauteed vegetables. Bake for an additional 30 minutes. Makes 1- 12" pizza.

Satisfying Paleo Snacks

Vegan-Paleo Spinach and Artichoke Dip

- 1 lb. spinach or baby spinach leaves

- 2 cans (14 oz. each) artichoke hearts in brine

- 1 cup diced onion

- 1 tbsp. olive oil

- 3 cloves garlic, peeled, crushed, and chopped finely

- 1/2 tsp. cayenne pepper

- 2 cups cashew cream

- juice of 1/2 a lemon

- dash of onion powder

- dash of garlic powder

- sea salt and pepper, to taste.

Rinse and thoroughly drain the spinach and set aside. Drain the artichokes and chop them well, but roughly.

In a small skillet, saute the onions until translucent, in the olive oil. Add the garlic and cook until fragrant. Add to the pan the artichoke hearts along with a dash of salt and pepper, garlic powder, onion powder, and cayenne, just until heated.

Add the spinach to the pan, along with the lemon juice. Stir until blended together. Finish by stirring in the cashew cream, along with any more salt and pepper to get the taste just the way you like it.

This dip is fabulous when served warm with vegetable slices and other dippable paleo-friendly treats.

Paleo Trail Mix

For an easy and delicious snack, mix together

- Macadamia nuts

- Walnuts

- Pecans

- Almonds

- Good quality dark chocolate chips (60% cacao and up)

- Pistachios

- Raisins

- And dried cherries (sulfur-free, unsweetened)

Get creative with your paleo diet friendly ingredients to create delicious and unique trail mixes that are ideal for snacking anytime, anywhere.

Kale Chips

1 bunch kale

Coconut oil

Sea salt

Garlic powder

Sesame seeds (optional).

Wash and thoroughly drain/dry the kale. Chop roughly and place on a cookie sheet. Lightly drizzle coconut oil over the kale chips, using your hands to spread it around to each piece.

Sprinkle the kale with sea salt and garlic powder and bake in a preheated 350 degree F oven for approximately 12-15 minutes, or until the edges of some of the leaves have turned a rustic brown. Turn the oven off, leaving the kale inside to dry out and cool in the oven.

Once the chips feel crispy to the touch, take them out of the oven. Immediately sprinkle with sesame seeds.

From Scratch Paleo Granola Bars

1 cup unsweetened coconut

2 tbsp grass-fed, organic, unsalted butter

1/3 cup local honey

2 tsp. real vanilla extract

1/2 cup roasted almonds, chopped roughly

1 cup walnuts, chopped

1/2 cup pecans, chopped roughly

1 cup roasted pumpkin seeds

3/4 cup raisins

1 1/2 tsp. cinnamon

Line an 8x8 baking pan with parchment paper and preheat the oven to 300 degrees F.

Thoroughly combine coconut, nuts, pumpkin seeds, raisins, and cinnamon in a large mixing bowl. Set aside.

Over medium heat in a sturdy saucepan, mix honey and butter until boiling, then continue cooking for one minute. Immediately pour into the bowl of dry ingredients, mixing thoroughly.

Put the mixture into the parchment lined baking pan, using a separate sheet of parchment paper to push the mixture evenly into the pan. Be sure the mixture has settled into the pan.

Bake in the 300 degree oven for 30 minutes. After they have cooled, the bars can be stored in the refrigerator overnight to

allow them to settle. The next day, cut the granola bars into ten equal bars-- and enjoy!

Desserts

Virgin Paleo Pina Colada

Juice of 1/2 a lime

1 ripe banana

1 cup fresh pineapple juice (no sugar added)

1 cup cold coconut milk

4-5 ice cubes

In a Blender, combine all ingredients until smooth. Pour into 2 small glasses and serve cold. Garnish with a chunk of fresh pineapple.

Paleo (and Vegan, AND Gluten Free) Divine Vanilla Cheesecake

In a food processor, pulse together

1/3 cup coconut flakes (unsweetened)

2 cups almond meal

4 large, pitted and destemmed dates

2 Tbsp. melted coconut oil, preferably organic

2 Tbsp. high quality maple syrup

Continue to pulse until the mixture is smooth- it's going to make your crust.

Line a glass pie dish with parchment paper and press the crust mixture evenly into the dish. Put the crust in the freezer to set

while you prepare your unbelievably delicious paleo, vegan, AND gluten free filling.

Soak 3 cups of cashews in a covered bowl filled with water for 3-4 hours. In your food processor, blend the cashews along with

The juice of 3 lemons

2/3 cup high quality maple syrup

1/2 tsp sea salt

1 1/2 tsp vanilla extract

seeds of one vanilla bean.

Once the mixture is creamy, add 3/4 cup melted coconut oil

Take the set crust out of the freezer and pour the well blended filling into the pan immediately. Ensure that the filling is evenly spread over each bit of crust. Return the pan to the freezer, allowing to set overnight or for at least 8 hours. No baking necessary! Just freeze and serve!

To make this cheesecake even better -if you can believe it- puree 2 1/2 cups of your favorite fresh fruit with maple syrup and serve drizzled over the top!

Paleo Brownies

Preheat oven to 350 degrees F. In a large mixing bowl, sift together:

4 Tbsp. almond flour

Sea salt

1/2 tsp baking powder

1/4 cup dutch cocoa powder (unsweetened)

In another mixing bowl combine

1 free range egg

3 Tbsp. raw, unfiltered honey

2 Tbsp. almond butter

1/2 cup vanilla flavored almond milk (unsweetened)

1 tsp. vanilla extract

Make sure the wet ingredients are mixed together thoroughly. Pour the bowl of wet ingredients into the large bowl with the dry ingredients. When the mixture is well combined, fold in

1/4 cup miniature organic dark chocolate chips

Pour brownie mixture into a glass baking dish. Bake in 350 degree F oven for 30-35 minutes, or until a cake tester (or toothpick) comes out clean.

Gorgeous Green Smoothie

1 cup coconut milk, chilled

Juice of 1/2 a lime

1 diced Kiwifruit, peeled

2 cups kale, chopped, stems removed

1 mango, prepared and diced

Put all ingredients together in a blender or food processor. Pulse and blend until well combined. Pour into a glass and enjoy.

Serves 2

Grilled Bananas

1 banana, cut in quarters, peel left on

Coconut oil, melted

Cinnamon

Maple syrup (optional)

While the grill or griddle is heating, brush the exposed sections of the banana quarters with coconut oil and sprinkle with cinnamon.

Grill with the peel facing up for 3-4 minutes, then flip and grill the bananas peel side down for an equal amount of time.

Immediately serve drizzled with maple syrup, if desired.

Mint Chocolate Paleo Shake

8 mint leaves

1 Tbsp. coconut syrup

2 Tbsp. melted dark chocolate (60% cacao)

1 cup coconut cream

handful of ice cubes

In a blender or food processor, combine all ingredients well to create a delicious grasshopper style shake. Makes one large shake..

About The Author

As a professionally trained triathlete and anthropology major, Ned Campbell is a dedicated advocate of the healthy and sustainable Paleo lifestyle. A native of the Colorado Rockies, Campbell originally discovered the Paleo diet during his father's battle with Parkinson's, and continues to spread the good word in the fight against degenerative diseases of all kinds.

An active outdoorsman and athlete, Campbell participated in endurance sports and training from a very early age, participating in his first marathon at 16. Though he would not go on to become a renowned professional athlete, his early love for health and fitness would continue into his college career and throughout his life. Armed with an education focused on indigenous North American peoples, Campbell began to incorporate his extensive knowledge of human history with a growing passion for sustainable health.

Campbell's true passion to bring physical wellbeing to everyone began with his father's Parkinson's diagnosis in 2002. The family tragedy caused by this degenerative disease pushed Campbell to research the natural cure and prevention of Parkinson's and other degenerative conditions.

Ned Campbell's strong personal philosophy combines a deep understanding of natural human history with an advanced personal interest in natural remedies, food cures, and overall good health. Campbell seeks to encourage healthy, sustainable eating habits in people of all ages and health situations. Recently, Campbell has focused his work on encouraging teens and young adults to use early preventative health practices, including the Paleo diet, to reduce the Alzheimer's rate in the US.

At home in his Colorado residence, Campbell prepares healthy Paleo dishes for his two sons and their beagle, Rosy..

Printed in Poland
by Amazon Fulfillment
Poland Sp. z o.o., Wrocław